At the Edge of
the Orchard
Country

Also by Robert Morgan

Zirconia Poems
Red Owl
Land Diving
Trunk & Thicket
Groundwork
Bronze Age

WESLEYAN POETRY

Robert Morgan

At the Edge of the Orchard Country

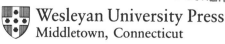
Wesleyan University Press
Middletown, Connecticut

Some of the poems in this book appeared originally in
*American Poetry Review, The American Scholar, Antaeus,
Bluefish, Bronze Age* (Iron Mountain Press), *Carolina
Quarterly, Chiaroscuro, Epoch, The Generation of 2000*
(Ontario Review Press), *Kenyon Review, New Virginia
Review, Ontario Review, Poetry Now, Seattle Review,
Science 84, The Small Farm, Songs from Unsung Worlds*
(Birkhauser), *Sparrow, Tendril, Three Sisters, Verse,
Virginia Quarterly Review.* "Horace Kephart," "White
Autumn," "Earth Closet," "Harrow," "Lost Colony,"
School Ground," "Nail Bag," "Visitors," "The Charge,"
and "Chant Royal" appeared first in *Poetry*.

The author would like to thank The National Endowment
for the Arts for a fellowship which was of great assistance
in the completion of this book.

LIBRARY OF CONGRESS CATALOGING-IN-
PUBLICATION DATA

Morgan, Robert, 1944–
    At the edge of the orchard country.
    (Wesleyan poetry)
    I. Title. II. Series.
PS3563.087147A8   1987   811'.54   85-29506
ISBN 0-8195-5158-9 (alk. paper)
ISBN 0-8195-6164-9 (pbk. : alk. paper)

All inquiries and permissions requests should be addressed
to the Publisher, Wesleyan University Press, 110 Mt.
Vernon Street, Middletown, Connecticut 06457.

Distributed by Harper & Row Publishers, Keystone
Industrial Park, Scranton, Pennsylvania 18512.

Manufactured in the United States of America

FIRST EDITION

Wesleyan Poetry

Contents

One

Two

Three

One

Horace Kephart

Outside the tent on the Little Fork
of the Sugar Fork of Hazel Creek
a man is writing. His table boards
on upended kegs, he drafts meticulously clear
paragraphs and weights the finished pages
with a shotgun shell. Squirrels rippling
in the trees above do not distract him.
The jug by a white pine is stopped with a cob.

Each sentence he scratches with economy
is payment on a vast unpayable obligation:
to his parents for the years of college, for
the special courses at Cornell, for his tenure
cataloguing Petrarch in Florence, for the girl,
his Laura, married in Ithaca and taken
west, for the librarian's post in St. Louis,
for the study of Finnish, for the unwritten
history of western exploration that
excused long camping holidays and nights
away from home and expensive rare editions,
for the weeks of drinking and sulk.

Lean as a mountaineer himself, galluses
swung at his sides, he scribbles to the young
his intensity of woodcraft, weapons, survival,
and of the hillmen his archaic friends and landlords,
makers of spirits. Even now one's loose
hog crashes through the brush into his camp

and knocks a tentline from its stob so
the canvas home sags at one corner on
his narrow cot, and breaks the clothesline.
As he jumps to shout and whack it back
into the undergrowth the unfinished sheet
from an early chapter of *Our Southern Highlanders*
peels off the desk and luffs like a wounded
dove out through scrub and leaves to the creek.

Passenger Pigeons

Remembering the descriptions by Wilson
and Bartram, and Audubon and other
early travelers to the interior, of the sky
clouded with the movements of winged pilgrims
wide as the Mississippi, wide as the Gulf
Stream, hundred-mile epics of equidistant wings
horizon to horizon, how their droppings
splashed the lakes and rivers, how
where they roosted whole forests broke down
worse than from ice storms, and the woods floor
was paved with their lime, how the settlers
got them with ax and gun and broom
for hogs, how when a hawk attacked
the endless stream bulged away
and kept the shift long after
the raptor was gone, and having read how
the skies of America became silent, the fletched
oceans forgotten, how can I replace
the hosts of the sky, the warm-blooded jetstreams?
To echo the birdstorms of those early
sunsets, what high river of electron, cell and star?

Buffalo Trace

Sometimes in the winter mountains
after a little snow has blown in the night
and nothing's alive in eye-range
but the clouds
near peaks frozen clean
in the solstice sun,
the white finds a faint depression
to stick in out of wind
and makes visible for the first time
through woods and along the slopes
to where it nicks the rim
perceptibly, a ghostpath
under brush and broomsedge,
merging in the pasture with narrow
cowtrails but running on through fences
and across boundaries, under branches
in tattered sweep out to the low
gaps of the old migrations
where they browsed into the summer mountains
then ebbed back into the horizon
and back of the stars.

Feather Bed

Sunk in feathers, head to the east,
the settler dreams of milkweed and warm blizzards,
drifting out on balconies of cloud.
Buried in the thistle he floats
on the frontier dark as though cradled
by great wings. Each tiny feather
writes its warmth and milk foams in the pail
brought over the mountains and over the whitewater,
as the wilderness roars and the sky shakes
its molt on hut and clearing ruts
and panther in the trees, making all pure,
lifting the whole territory back
over the hills and piedmont and tidewater,
across the troubled Atlantic and centuries
toward a white immaculate garden.

Looking Homeward

Quiet as a photograph, the early
Sunday morning in Brooklyn, down miles
of doorways and closed shops, except
a dog worrying the garbage cans
in the alley behind a grocery, and in
the kitchen of an apartment
six feet below the street the scratch
of pen on paper. A giant in undershirt
and suspenders bends his tiny head
under the lamp and scrawls
enormous script, brushing the pages
to the already cluttered floor,
and pausing just long enough to number
the next, continues the rush of the sentence.
All chairs and boxes in the room
are buried in manuscript. The typist, when
she arrives after he's asleep, will have to
gather and collate. This night alone
he splashed down thirty thousand
words, as though digging out some vein
in a mountain at the peak of gold fever.
A dozen reams wait beside him to be fed
to his right hand. Another page slides
off the table and settles to the floor
like an October leaf in the room blue
with haze as a mountain autumn. He rubs
out a cigarette and, cursing the pen,
fills it from a jar and starts again,

lusting to sweep out across the virgin space
like an explorer leaving the scripture
of signs over the acres and acres
claimed by this deed of writing.

Eight hundred miles to the south and west
as the crow might dream or the flying machine
travels or the train goes rumbling through small
towns in the small hours of Sunday mornings
and ascends the long grade out of the Piedmont
to the hills, another hulk of human earth,
great belly punching through a filthy undershirt
and spread galluses, squats in a remote
cove to the eye of a doubler and catches
some drops in a gourd. The fire under the drum
of mash roars too hot for the season and for
the process, but he cannot keep himself
from feeding hardwood to the fire's claw.
The smoke alone would betray him but for
the Blue Ridge fogs, and the crackle is muffled
by the nearby waterfall. His rifle lies in the leaves.
He brushes aside hair straight and dark as a
Cherokee's and tastes from the gourd again, throws
the rest back into the tub under the spout.
When the fire dies he'll have to dump it all
back in the still for another run.
Once he glances back at the trail and at
the dozen barrels of mash jeweling the hollow
with sour. Above the fire and simmering waterfall

he seems to hear—something odd, and reaches
for the gun. Crouching at the edge of the laurel
he aims down the trail. Was it steps, or the
static of boiling water? Early sun sprays the opening
from windows in the canopy. He hears it again,
some ways down the valley, a woodpecker knocking timber,
each lick distinct as his heartbeat but signifying
only itself and empty woods. And miles beyond
a church bell echoes as though from inside a ridge.
He takes the ax and begins splitting more
oak for his and his neighbors' thirst.

Halley's Comet

"Look there," she said and pointed,
so he followed her arm out to where
the finger touched something delicate as a mayfly
wing in the evening sky, floating
neither blown nor fluttering. "It won't come
again for more than seventy years, and by then
I'll be gone but you might see it return."

That was in the yard of the old log barn
at milking time, and though she died within
the year of measles, the thing lit by her finger
stayed vivid for him long after the stalls
and all the stock were gone. He often tried
to recall what she said it portended: flood?
famine? war? It was nothing good.

It was a thing he looked forward to and feared,
for if he saw its milky breath again he'd be eighty-one,
and the century old and time's conclusion
near, for all preachers agreed the century would see
the end of this dimension. Some mighty
event came every two thousand years they said,
and he'd seen the signs himself in war and hatred.

But even in his fear he liked to think
the comet a kind of promise of the continuance
of things in a broken world—
the luminous streamer out there even now
sweeping back toward the sun and earth to light
the air like a nymph of yet another spring he'd been
privileged to remember her black eyes and pale hand.

White Autumn

She had always loved to read, even
in childhood during the Confederate War,
and built the habit later of staying up
by the oil lamp near the fireplace after
husband and children slept, the scrub-work done.
She fed the addiction in the hard years
of Reconstruction and even after
her husband died and she was forced
to provide and be sole foreman of the place.
While her only son fought in France
it was this second life, by the open window
in warm months when the pines on the hill
seemed to talk to the creek, or katydids
lined-out their hymns in the trees beyond the barn,
or by the familiar of fire in winter,
that sustained her. She and her daughters
later forgot the time, the exact date,
if there was such a day, she made her decision.
But after the children could cook
and garden and milk and bring in a little
by housecleaning for the rich in Flat Rock,
and the son returned from overseas
wounded but still able and married a war widow,
and when she had found just the right chair,
a rocker joined by a man over on Willow
from rubbed hickory, with cane seat and back,
and arms wide enough to rest her everlasting cup
of coffee on, or a heavy book,

she knew she had come to her place and would stay.
And from that day, if it was one time and not
a gradual recognition, she never crossed a threshold
or ventured from that special seat of rightness,
of presence and pleasure, except to be helped to bed
in the hours before dawn for a little nap.
That chair—every Christmas someone gave her a bright
cushion to break in—was the site on which she bathed
in a warm river of books and black coffee,
varieties of candy and cakes kept in a low cupboard
at hand. The cats passed through her lap and legs
and through the rungs of her seat. The tons
of firewood came in cold and left as light, smoke, ash.
She rode that upright cradle to sleep
and through many long visits with tiers of family,
kissing the babies like different kinds of fruit.
Always hiding the clay pipe in her cabinet
when company appeared. She chaired decisions
to keep the land and refused welfare.
On that creaking throne she ruled a tiny kingdom
through war, death of kin. Even on the night she did
stop breathing, near a hundred, no one knew
exactly when, but found the lamp still on,
the romance open to a new chapter,
and the sun just appearing at her elbow.

Two

Books in the Attic

Sunday afternoon we crossed the branch
and climbed by the molasses furnace
to the springhouse with its melodic
pipe, past the smokehouse full of spider-
shrouded jars, to the Morgan house.
Dozens had been born and died there,
but it stood a husk of sagging sills
and porch and damp echoing rooms
waiting to be wrecked. A barn lantern
had rusted crisp, the glass held by
a crust of metal. All of Daddy's
renovations before the war
for his bride were peeling, moldy.
In the closet we pulled ourselves
up the green-stepped ladder into
atticlight. There, scattered by owls
and nesting squirrels whose cobs remained,
sprawled the books of the family
smelling of must and old tobacco,
silverfish and pages singed by time,
the fat histories Great-grandpa
got in Augusta when he wagoned
hams and produce down the Winding Stairs.
Loose sheets spiced the floor with pale ink:
vague photographs of Teddy
Rough Rider, worm-hollowed magazines
and rifle catalogues, pencil
accounts. Boots molded to the corns

and toes of dead plowmen slouched in
a bronzing of dust. The pages seemed
to hover, unfolding wings and
facets to the light. A stout
Assyrian lion reared on the back
of an ancient history. We turned
the aromatic leaves like flakes
of boiled down and pressed extract
of the last century, until
my nose began to drip with the
so-far-unnoticed cold and there
was just light to see the ladder
down to the trail and milking time.

Ancient

By the end of summer the big weeds
outside the curve are heavy
with dust; you wonder how they stand.
Burdock drags to the ground

as after a snowstorm,
dirt even ridging its stems.
The joe-pye heads are powdered
and the teasel chalky as a miller's

eyebrows. The frailest limbs
have dumped their burdens several times
since the last rain. Wind
which otherwise would shake them clean

only settles on. You could believe
the ragweed and thistle had stood centuries
in a tomb, except the soot
still blooms where a bee digs into it.

Yellow

May is the yellow month. At this
latitude the woods are a fog of different
yellow-greens as first leaves
open pages and new twigs on the willows
grow bright as chicken fat.
In every yard the daffodils and dandelions,
and clouds of wild mustard light
the open fields, even as wind
bruises cowlicks in the rye. Along
highways and parks forsythia
sprays its heat, and fire rinses seedbeds
of old stalks at dark. The day begins
in a golden antiquity, flushing
the ridges so they echo inside the room
where flesh stretches into flower, where
even the interior of night is saffroned
the most erotic color of touch and know.

Manure Pile

Heaped gold and powerful behind the barn.
The crust, faded by weather, almost
never freezes, steaming off snow with the fever
of its inner work. Birds worry
the seeds exposed by rain.
Black chemistry of the core
nurses weeds on the baked hide
while the yard is frost-dead. Once
a little chick peeped from its straw
in January, hatched by the warmth.
The matter dug from its side for fields
is too strong even for worms to live in,
sealed years by the ammonia.
Haunted in the hot months by a genie
of flies, it jewels the downwind.
Sundays the many purple butterflies
that suck its inks, shiver off into the sky
where carillons of convection ring.

Bonus

In the little summer after Indian Summer,
sun instead of snow returns
and day by day the west breathes warm
through weeds frost-withered a month.
In this spell, dead fields and
woods drab onto the perfect sky.
And sudden dandelions flare
in grass. Even the banks
of brown goldenrod find sap and bloom again
over mud and the rot-ink of ditches,
as mice and shrews hurry for seeds.
Thistle molts in the quiet,
for most birds have gone.
What feast days! to salvage
among the trash and ruins, where
ice tooth and snow should be fasting.

Brownian Motion

The air is an aquarium where
every mote spins wild
and prisms the morning light.
Lint climbs sparkling on
convection's fountain,
and magnetic storms boil away
like gnats bumped by molecules.
Every breath swarms
the clear spores, ion seethe,
magnified in playful flight.
Look at the dust panic
off a fingertip. Each
particle is an opal angel
too small to see but in the glare
of this annunciation.

Lightning Bug

Carat of the first radiance,
you navigate like a creature
of the deep. I wish I could read
your morse across the night yard.
Your body is a piece of star
but your head is obscure. What small
photography! What instrument
panel is on? You are winnowed
through the hanging gardens of night.
Your noctilucent syllables
sing in the millennium of
the southern night with star-talking
dew, like the thinker sending nous
into the outerstillness from
the edge of the orchard country.

Dead Dog on the Highway

Looks already part of the shoulder
mess, assimilated into weeds and tire-peels,
ditch trash. Swollen tight and gray
with diesel grime before we find him,
who loved to fanfare every truck on the dirt road
below the house but had no way to judge
the speed of oncoming playmates
on the wide-lane. The transfer
must have seemed to break from its future
at him. The brake skids show
how far the rig's momentum slapped him
in the last and longest leap of a life
of running cars and fieldmice. Someone
has burst a Falstaff bottle
so he wears a halo of crushed ice.
He looks frozen in mid-gallop except
for the wrongness of the broken back.
The paw pads you want to caress
they're so familiar. A fang exposed
through the sooty underlip bites turf.
Traffic shivers the dirty fur and ear tip.
No blood shows, though ants are busy with the eyes.
The body is so heavy we feel it
must be glued to the dirt as we drag
it to the hole in the embankment,
as though dead flesh having found its bed
would stay there until it soaks
into the topsoil and rots a fume
across the hunting weather.

Bare Yard

My grandma swept her yard
often as the floor
and wore out willow switches
and swatches of broomsedge
sewn in bundles
to whisk away the twigs
and pebbles, leaves and chicken piles.
She washed down the soiled places
with buckets from the spring
and sprinkled branch sand
over any chicken tracks or stains
that might show through,
and brushed it clean as snow.
How fresh the yard looked then.
You didn't want to track
the virgin cover so white,
so perfect a sheet sparkling
with quartz and mica, and kept
to the edges of the boxwoods.
The yard was isled with tufts
of grass near its borders.
Grandma placed her geraniums out there
in their brick-clay pots.

The ground looked plain and hard
as her expression while she worked.
Cropped grass was for the pasture
and graveyard and meadow.
She set a few gourds and unusual
rocks by the steps and flowerbeds.
Otherwise the space was bare and bright
in the sun as her conscience.

Radio

In the corner farthest from the fire,
a safe of carved oak,
cabinet of voices.
The gothic windows stretched with cloth
hide a powerful hum when Grandpa
rolls the knob and the numbers
light up as the needle
passes in its window.
He hunts for the combination.
Birds back somewhere among
the preachers, static, whine
and whistle late at night from forests.
I want to reach in there
and find the jars that sing,
and watch through a gap in the back
the vials glowing in the muck of wires,
a throbbing in the metal
where the languages of the air
are trapped and spoken.
That space unreachable in the small light,
poisoned by electricity.

The Gift of Tongues

The whole church got hot and vivid
with the rush of unhuman chatter
above the congregation,
and I saw my father looking at
the altar as though electrocuted.
It was a voice I'd never heard
but knew as from other centuries.
It was the voice of awful fire.
"What's he saying?" Ronald hissed
and jabbed my arm. "Probably Hebrew."
The preacher called out another
hymn, and the glissade came again,
high syllables not from my father's
lips but elsewhere, the flare of
higher language, sentences of light.
And we sang and sang again, but
no one rose as if from sleep to
be interpreter, explain the writing
on the air that still shone there like
blindness. None volunteered a gloss
or translation or receiver
of the message. My hands hurt
when pulled from the pew's varnish
they'd gripped and sweated so. Later,
standing under the high and plain-
sung pines on the mountain I clenched
my jaws like pliers, holding in
and savoring the gift of silence.

Bellrope

The line through the hole in the dank
vestibule ceiling ended in
a powerful knot worn slick, swinging
in the breeze from those passing. Half
an hour before service Uncle
Allen pulled the call to worship,
hauling down the rope like the starting
cord of a motor, and the tower
answered and answered, fading
as the clapper lolled aside. I watched
him before Sunday school heave on
the line as on a wellrope. And
the wheel creaked up there as heavy
buckets emptied out their startle
and spread a cold splash to farthest
coves and hollows, then sucked the rope
back into the loft, leaving just
the knot within reach, trembling
with its high connections.

Parlor

No one ever glimpsed Aunt Florrie's
livingroom, not even the preacher
when he came for yearly Sunday
dinner, maybe not even Uncle
John, in the later years of their
marriage. Watching her scrub down
the clapboards of porch and house
with rag and pail I thought about
the interior that seemed to signal
its gloom from behind lace curtains
and windows closed against all dust.
How did the holy of holies
look, her whatnots and china,
chair legs and clocks, gleaming so
you could count every piece of dust
in the shadows? As her husband
and sons tramped in from the fields and
stable, washed at the backdoor pump,
she wiped on her knees the facets of
that isolated crystal each
morning and afternoon, polishing
its virgin completeness like some
last remnant of Eden, a room
amid the dirt and accident
of her world and time already
set aside like a closet of
the future, dustless heaven.

Potato Hole

Just big enough to give spuds a warm burial
and smother bulbs and apples to sleep,
in a houseless cellar decorated by mold
like an Etruscan tomb. I've hid out
there on a windy day riding out a peeve
and eating winesaps, watching dust wrestle

in the light from the keyhole above. What
shelter below the floor of storm. Are those
in graves happy as me on a blustery day
rubbing an apple new? The weather up there
harries livestock, outbuildings, people. Governments
threaten war but I lounge on that

bumpy harvest and dream of staying in my
fundamental lair till spring and emerging
strong and applefed after all is blown away.
I'll rise with the first shoots
of Lazarus green. Beneath the hearth of frost
such heaps of nuggets, sweet and Irish,

and the smell of leaves we lined the bed with.
Snow crackles on the wooden door above
and seeps a few flakes through the pore
like bits of opium. I float
in my capsule among the stars, beyond,
where the only dirt is me and mine.

Sunday Toilet

On the hottest Sundays of the year,
in the morning shift of bird hymn
and dew song, before the church bell
split the poised whole, Daddy raked
a waterbucket full of lime
from the pile beside the toolshed
and flung comets and smoking hands
on the walls of the hogpen.
The young shoat's feet sucked mud as he
ran to corners from the fog that
flurried over sty and ripening
puddles and drifted on the spillage
of cobs rotting on the downhill side.
The dusting finished, the pen looked
white as confectioner's sugar
in the cooling talc, the whiteness
somehow medicinal if not
opiate, and the air was
sweeter floating up to the house
where the preacher would come to dinner.
After the hogpen Daddy sprinkled
the chicken yard and floor of the
brooder house, dropped what was left
down the holes of the two-seat
toilet. When the make-up was hit

by early sun the mire looked
pristine and cool as the tops of
cumulus reaching to heaven
while women powdered their faces
for church and flies got chalk on their
feet to write on the back screen door.

Cowbedding

Grandma broke a forked stick and raked
the leafpack into little heaps
like treasure—frost
gluing the rotten scraps beneath
to earth. What smell of oak tobacco,
woodmusk. The top leaves crisp as laundry.
I want to go back there and help
hold the sack open while she
feeds the burlap hands of gold
and stuffs in more,
inflating the rough cloth.
I put my hands to the last
pile as to a fire.
Opened in the stall and shaken,
the udders spray leaves
over the manure.
The bare patches we left thawing
in the woods were bigger than the stall,
wider than the barn floor,
and looked like yards swept for a dance
or maybe threshing. I want to go
back and stand on the frost
of their spelled circles,
and gather the clean money of the trees
for clothes, for my pillow.

Hay Scuttle

The holes in the floor of the barn loft
were cut for dropping shucks to the stalls.
Pile an armload on the opening
and stuff them through. The cow
is already eating as the rest
splash on her head. The fodder sweet
as tobacco is pushed down for the horse.
Light from below rises with manure
and warm cud-breath.
And bleach from the horse's bed.
Dark up here with the dead grass
and cornsheller, except for the trapdoors.
Only way out to the sun is down,
through the exquisite filth.

Earth Closet

Not much bigger than a dollhouse raised
in the hemlock shade,
the out-closet greens with moss.
The door opens on a chest with holes
and closes on a booth of calling space.
The spiders in corners are affluent with flies.
Needles seep through the cracks and have to be
swept from the seats.
Look down into the lime-frozen pit.
Except for the creak of the spruce pine
polishing the roof, you're alone
with the pause of earth—hillflesh
raw beneath. The enhoused shrine
spreads batter downhill crusting at the edges,
becoming dirt. Smell of the dank catalogue.
The excess is thrown as in a wishing pool
and, the daily toll of soil rendered
to soil in the rites of earth,
the watchman's box is left
its closeness inside the weather.

Harrow

This was my first plowing, to step
behind a drag alone holding
the long sweat-heavy lines and lean
to gee and haw. No harm could be
except to draw the horse in too
close a turn and snarl hooves in the
traces and singletree, for
the field was just turned and the rye
broken by the moldboard drying
in hawsers of clods that needed
tearing and cutting, plain wearing away.
So I circled the acre in
shrinking rounds, playing the mare like
a heavy kite that bumped and lurched
into the March sky as I crossed
the ridge and, turning, stood on the
harrow frame downhill as the spikes
bit into the stubble and combed
out the worm-shiny clods. The world
that spring afternoon was drying
out and needed grooming and
leveling and smoothing until
it shone velvet for the laying
off and seed. And I held in soaked
palms one great smelly horsepower
that leapt ahead to my voice
and sideways toward the eye of
the planet's newest field.

Coccidiosis

The cloud of white leghorns in the lot
looked broken up and dirty, old.
The once-fat pullets got scrawny
and the straw nests in the house stayed
empty every day of all
except the cold china eggs. My
parents had borrowed to buy the
brooder house and brooder and mail-sent
chicks. It was their scheme, suggested
by the county agent, to have
income through the Cold War winters.
With euphoria we'd watched the biddy
puffs of yellow grow up and white
and then get snowy feathers. But
as the laying started and we
thought the hard years done, it ended
and the layers wasted empty.
They shed and where the skin showed the rest
pecked until the flock was bloody.
The county agent sent a man
who probed and prodded for an hour,
then washed his hands and said they'd have
to die: coccidiosis.
A million parasites in each
had cut their guts to holes and no
eating could help. Expensive mash
bought on credit would not feed or
make an egg. Their bodies were not

fit for frying. That afternoon
we chopped off every head and filled
a pit in the garden with our
white investment. And later learned
the county agent had started so
many others in the business
even those with eggs could not sell
and fryers brought less than they took
to feed. The government's best
efforts had made a thousand families
poorer beyond the ordinary.
Our loss had been instant was all.

Throwing Rocks

At the age of nine or ten I would stand
in the road a whole afternoon, stepping
back to choose a perfect rock, then
running almost to the weeds and sailing
it over the pasture. Thumb and brown
index finger wore rough and my arm loosened

in its socket. The sleeve got ragged from
the whipping action. But what a joy
to feel the stone soar out like a part
of me, riding the afternoon's alloy
of light in a long curve to find and hit
the gully by the branch. I was at home

in the scatter of gravel at my feet,
knowing just where the next flat one lay,
working gradually back, messing the bed
with tracks and dislodged rejects. I could play
all the parabolas of air that spread
over the field and fence and pasture, alert

the instant I'd released a throw down valley
if the spin would keep it level and if
the arc was right to reach the branch. I flung
away the road, getting closer, but off
the gleam of water until a faint ring
swelled from the bull's-eye of victory.

Intent on length and accuracy of each throw
I was astonished when a car rattled by
so close it almost brushed me, and found
where I was and that I was only me
and not the fierce searching around
the gravel for the best dusty ammo

to glide like dollars across the blue
and the sight running out my sore wing
and off the guiding finger on the air
to a distant splash or, closer, thudding
into the brush and weeds and branch mire.
I had other loves also, and work to do.

Elmer's Seat

Elmer sits for years on the bank
above the meadow, watching his
cow graze. There is a seat pressed in
the leaves that seems the bed of some
animal scooped out of the hill
and shaded by the margin oaks
and white pine grove. The nest is both
leaf-lined and needle-cushioned, new
with every wind. He grazes
his cow in the spring-glade and watches
her hour by hour and afternoon
by afternoon, not moving, still as
when he lay two days in Flanders
mud and bodies, playing his corpse
and watching the sky change sides. Ground
squirrcls work around and rabbits
and woodpeckers gather and leave
while hepaticas shine and leaf
out into summer as he looks
and the Jersey changes spots and
trees color and airplanes get higher
above and quieter until
they are almost invisible
except for cobwebs floating down.

Uncle Robert

M Sgt. Robert G. Levi 1915–1943
Serial No. 34119284
813th Bomb Sqdn.
482nd Bombardment Group
Eighth Air Force

In the little opening in the woods
your cot springs were a crisp red wool
on the moss. While we raked leaves
for the cowstall Grandma told me how
you came up here on summer afternoons
to read and paint and sleep after
working the hootowl shift at the cottonmill.
You must have meant to return to leave
your couch on the innerspring moss
on the mountainside.

      The metalwork you did
in the CCC—toolbox, a vase, buckets
thick as stoves—was scattered through house
and barn. I lost your flies and tackle
in the weeds above the garden, and stuck
your chevron patches to my flannel shirt.
In the messkit returned from England
I fried sand like snow, and found
the picture of your fiancée in the cedarchest.

It was hinted I was "marked" somehow,
not only by your name, but in some way
unexplained was actually you. Aunts and cousins
claimed we favored and I spoke with your stammer.
Your paintings watched me
from the bedroom wall and mantel
and your poem clipped from the paper
yellowed among the rationbooks. I inherited
your Testament with its boards of carved cedar,
and the box of arrowheads you picked
from the dust of bottomlands on Sunday afternoons
like seeds and teeth of giants.

No one opened the steel coffin sent back
to see what bone splinters or rags
had been found where the B-17 novaed
above East Anglia. I touched the ribbons
and medals in the bureau, the gold buttons.
Your canoe lay in the barnloft for years
between the cornpile and the wall, heavy
with dust as the boat in a pyramid
and tracked by mice and swallows. The paint
and canvas curled away from the cedar slats.
I meant to use it someday but never dared:
it was not creekworthy without new skin
and too heavy for one to carry. I turned
it over and looked into the belly
and sat on the webbed seat, rocking

on the corn-bearinged floor. Once hornets
built in the prow what I imagined
was a skull with honey brains. On snowy days
I sat there and paddled across the wilderness
of loft dark. The summer before you left
you portaged to the river and back,
then carried the canoe up there.
Something was always scary about the craft:
each time I turned it over fearing to see
a body inside. It lay among the shucks
and fodder as though washed up by a flood
and stranded forever.

                         One day I found your bugle
in the attic, velveted with dust and lint.
The brass felt damp with corrosion,
the bell dented and dark as leather.
I took it out behind the house and,
facing west, blew into the cold mouthpiece
a hopeful syllable. The metal trembled
and blared like a sick steer, went quiet.
I poured all my body heat into the barrel
and a sour flatulence shook out and echoed
off the mountains. I made half-musical
squeaks and bursts till dizzy, aiming vowels
like watermelon seeds into the tube.
When the groans returned from Buzzard Rock
I thought they must be wails from the cove

for someone dead, and nothing I had sent,
or the ghost of a train lost in the valley
and relayed like an aural mirage from
the past still with us and talking back.

The flag that draped your casket was kept
folded in the trunk. They said
I had the high-arched "Levi foot"
like you, and your quick laugh. I was told
you made your own marbles as a boy
by rolling branch clay into balls and baking
in the oven. Mama liked to take out
of cloth a clay statue of a naked man
face down in the dirt which you once
modeled and called "The Dying Warrior."
I marveled at the cunning work of leg
and tiny arm and spilling hair, and touched
your fingerprints still clear on the base.

Firecrackers at Christmas

In the Southern mountains, our big
serenade was not the Fourth but
always Christmas Eve and Christmas.
Starting at midnight the valleys
and branch coves fairly shook with barks
of crackers, boom of shotguns, jolt
even of sticks of dynamite.
You would have thought a new hunting
season had begun in the big-star
night, or that a war had broken
out in the scattered hollows: all
the feuds and land disputes come to
a magnum finale. The sparks
everywhere of match and fuse
and burst were like giant lightning bugs.
Thunder doomed the ridges though
the sky shone clear and frost sugared
the meadows. Yankees were astonished
at the violence and racket
on the sacred day, they said, as
cherrybombs were hurled into yards
and placed expanding mailboxes
same as Halloween. Perhaps the custom
had its origins in peasant-pagan
times of honoring the solstice
around a burning tree, or in
the mystery centuries of

saluting the miraculous
with loudest brag and syllable.
Certainly the pioneer had
no more valuable gift to bring
than lead and powder to offer
in the hush of hills, the long rifles
their best tongues for saying the peace
they claimed to carry to the still
unchapeled wilderness, just as
cannon had been lit in the Old
World to announce the birth of kings.
They fired into the virgin skies
a ceremony we repeated
ignorantly. But what delight
I felt listening in the unheated
bedroom dark, not believing in
Santa Claus or expensive gifts,
to the terrible cracks along
the creek road and up on Olivet,
as though great rivers of ice were
breaking on the horizon and
trees were bursting at the heart
and new elements were being born
in whip-stings and distant booms
and the toy chatter of the littlest
powder grace notes. That was our
roughest and best caroling.

Man and Machine

Besides drinking and telling lies,
nothing interested my cousin Luther
like working with the tractor.
Astride that bright and smelly beast
he was a man inspired.
Revving and tearing the stubble
of early spring he cussed
the metal like a favorite mule,
parrying any stallout with the shift.
In too big a hurry to turn
at the end of a row he jammed
in a brake and spun around,
lowered the harrows
into the winter-bleached field
and blasted off for yon end.
Barely able to read, he took
dusters and bush hogs and diesel movements
apart with the skill of a surgeon,
hollering on the phone for parts
as far away as Charlotte or Atlanta.
Would stay on his ass at the filling station
or country store for weeks
while wife and kids and parents
picked in the heat the crops he'd
drive to market. Neither storm-threat
nor overripening could move him
to join their labor. Until time
for dusting with the homemade blower

mounted on a jeep. Or after the vines
were cut he'd windlass in the long wires.
Winters Luther lived only for his truck,
banging down the dirt road to Chestnut Springs
for booze and women. But that was just
occasional. Most days he'd brag at the store
about his pickup, or be trading for another
with even thicker tires, more horsepower
and chrome, a gunrack in the window.
At home he'd maybe tune a little,
oil the plates of the planter.
But off the machine he was just
another stocky hoojer, yelling
to make up for his lack of size
and self-esteem, adding fat and blood
pressure. Late February breaking time
transformed him. He leapt on the big
diesel and burned out its winter farts
all the way to the bottoms, whipping
the animal until it glowed, became
his legs and voice and shoulders.
To children and himself he tore up ground
like a centaur. Plowing with the lights on
all night in the river fields
he circled more times than any race driver,
shouting in the settling damp while
we slept hearing the distant fury.
And by morning the fields were new.

Cleaning Off the Cemetery

Not the church-devout but those
reverent to family memory
show for these workings held
every three to five springs,
some driving a ways, complaining,
but always here on the chosen day
with tools and kids and dinner.
Each starts by mowing off the plot
of kin, raising toppled stones,
filling a grave where the box
collapsed after its allotted years,
leaning bricks in a little fence
around an infant's burial.
But the margins, medians, vacant
sections for the future, and the spaces
of forgotten families, take
the real work. The woods
have to be cut back across the ground
they've claimed, a drain
mattocked out for the road.
Brush bound by honeysuckle must be ripped
off stones, and poison ivy
raked into the hidden gully,
while other trash is burned.
Broken glass and jars half-filled
with rotten flowers and toy lambs
are thrown away. Widening the parking lot

they find a skull where the slave
ground must have been. They
tell the young the harsh old times,
lean on scythes thinking how much care
the dead get, how few snakes they've killed
this year, and how this high reservoir
above the floods gets more work
than their yards in payment
for bringing all together.

Three

Lost Colony

The first spring they watched the east every day
for the ships, and planted what seed they
had saved from mold and rot in the island
sand with fish as the heathen had said.

But even by the sea it rained little
and their island gave just a trickle
of fresh water. Many died of fever
or bad air, especially children and expectant

wives. Evenings in the stockade
they prayed for the Captain to return with bread.
A cow was stolen by the Lumbees,
or maybe Croatans—by day professing

friendship, even interest in the Faith.
Often the men rowed out into the Sound
to fish and look for higher ground
up the tidal creeks, and found only

further marshes, a catarrh of mud squeezed
out of reeds, and alligators
bellowing in brakes. Two died of snakebite
while inspecting a hummock above the flats.

The season came foul again. One saw
in a dream their Knight beheaded in the Tower.
By Christmas with the biscuit gone
and powder for their fusils, the meager

magazines of grain now bare, they lived,
the dozen left, by snaring an occasional
duck, or fishing when the cold wind
abated and they could take oars

to the deep channels of the Sound.
And entered the new year, Indians now
paddling to their shore and mocking
with baskets of maize to be exchanged

for wives and daughters. An elder
ordered they start rowing in the skiff
for England and at least die bravely at sea,
not teased by infidels

and hunger tempting with each other's flesh,
nor wandering the wilderness to the west
where they understood the Spanish had,
through sin's alchemy, extracted base gold.

School Ground

First churches they put on the most
infertile ground, choosing a washed-
out Old Field of clay and broomsedge
or a hillside wrinkled with
erosion and baked by sun until
it showed quartz bones and every
pebble stood pedestaled on dirt.
For the good land, the greasy swamp
and floury bottom soil along
creeks, humus-brown forest floors and
gentle flanks of hills, must be cleared
for planting, and the shady places
around springs and the benchlands, used
for houses, woodpiles, feedlots. Leaving
only poorest soil for schoolhouse
and meetinghouse, showing how little
learning needed except the rod,
and how little this world had to do
with the next except as staging ground.
And these high bare spots if not tracks
of the gods as Indians had said
were at least scorched by many lightnings
and, so, blessed by both nakedness
and danger. And the crops of that
bad acre were a little knowledge
by heart, and souls, and what was planted
here to music and said lessons

took root hereafter. And every year
for centuries the grass would be
manured with those who had sung and
recited here until it would
become the valley's greenest tilth.

Nail Bag

When a cleared farm wore out or washed
in three to seven years, the soil
bleached and threadbare, they just burned the barn
down for the nails and moved on,
wagon banging buckets, babies
howling, oxen straining at fords
and ridges. To the next claim. And
once the trees on that acreage were
girdled and felled, they burned the logs
and plowed the ashes around stumps,
bringing in enormous yields from
the singed ground. Then took out the sack
of nails like slivers of crystal
that hammered right would summon
wilderness into new structure.
As though all husbandry and home
were carried in that charred handful
of iron stitches, blacksmithed chromosomes
that link distant generations.

Visitors

The ground is haunted by the Cherokee.
Ashes, teeth of arrows, pottery
work up in the Old Fields. Digging
for ginseng I'm afraid of cutting
a rotted hand. Half the boulders seem
scratched with messages. Over the rim
of the Craggies clouds lift signals.
In company with word and star all
weeds are medicine. The rivers
have names they repeat forever
just out of hearing. A doe
shows her thigh through the shadows.
The names Saluda, Oklawaha run
a secret stairway of the spine.
What one deity shall we
raise to speak to their powerful many?

Jutaculla Rock

Up in Jackson County they have
this soapstone in a field, scored all over
with hieroglyphics no one has solved.
Or maybe it's more picture writing,
the figures so rough and worn
they no longer represent. But
the markings are at least distinct
enough to tell they're made with hands
and not just thaw and wind and water.
Among the written characters of all creation
that big rock seems significant, but
like the written characters of all
creation is unintelligible without
a key to its whorls and wisps
of scipture that seem to shiver
in the rain on its face
like fresh-ink chromosomes
or voice-prints of quasars, there
in the washed-out cornfield. But what
could be more awesome than a message
ancient, untranslatable, true,
up where giants walked on the balds,
in text and context, history, word?

The Charge

On first coming to the ridges,
washed up on this wild, high shore
from lowland debt, indenture, this
one stayed his first year in a tree,
the story was. I see him clothed
in beard and hair and hides, asleep
on his rifle and feet, a quick
pith warming the trunk through the long
winter. Far above him bees have
filled the hulk with honey that drips
into his cell. In storms the living
tower creaks and he may remember
castles or months of his passage
here. He fits the hollow like a charge
unfired, the heart figure of rage
and hunger that will shoot and chop
and burn and plant his way across
the slopes when he wakens some morning
in late winter and sees thaw-light
and his own stained hands throwing
the shadow of all he is and
needs to lay the wilderness
except a woman's cooking spoon.

Chant Royal

Born in a notch of the high mountains where
a spring ran from under the porch, on
the second of April just one hundred years
ago this month, my grandpa was a weak one
to start with, premature, weighed a scant
two pounds twelve ounces. So fragile the aunt
who tended that first night feared to move
him except for feeding and the placing of
diapers. He slept near the fire in a shoebox
with one end cut out. Against the odds he would prove
adequate for survival, withstanding all knocks.

Because he was puny his mother would rear
him sheltered, keep him beside her out of the sun
and rain alike, feed him molasses and sulfur in fear
of worms and would let him walk, not run,
to the gap with the others to stand on the slant
bars while the cows were milked in elegant
twilight. Pious and hard, she showed her love
through strictness and was known to reprove
him for the least resistance. She tried raw fox
grape juice and teas of the yarb grannies, strove,
adequate for survival, withstanding all knocks,

to find faith healers, quacks, to cure
her youngest. A cousin wrote of Dr. Wilson
down near Greenville. They took the wagon one clear
morning and reached the town just as the moon

rose full. The man at the door said, "I can't
see you this late," but examined and began to rant
on the virtues of tobacco ("Give him a chew"), then shove
and shoo them out. That night they drove
all the way back. No telling what unlocks
vitality: from that day he began to grow and rove
adequate for survival, withstanding all knocks.

Frampold as any mountain branch, he hunted bees and deer,
carried to mill on Cold Friday and learned the fun
of shivarees and drinking. Saw his father appear
walking through the pasture toward him and beckon,
then vanish when he spoke like any haint,
and die within the month. He heard a panther
scream and follow as he came back through the cove
from hogkilling, and sat up nights by the stove
while his brother crisised with the fever and tried to mock
death before it cooled him. Nobody who saw the dove
was adequate for survival, withstanding all knocks.

Out sanghunting he met Mrs. Capps and her
daughter sawing crosscut. The girl could stun
with her beauty, hiding bare feet under leaves. Inner
currents stirred. He quit drinking, came to church, and won
her after three weeks' courting. But they lived in want
the first year; a child died. He made his covenant

one cold night in the orchard and a trove
came in acres for sale cheap on the creek above
the Andrews place. There he sank a well through rock,
weathered debt, depression, set groves,
adequate for survival, withstanding all knocks.

Envoi

Guardian ghost, inhere herein. Before Jove
may this music honor his example, improve
my time as he invested his, and no less unorthodox
discover significance in the bonds his fate wove
adequate for survival, withstanding all knocks.

Field Theory

In those days they grew sweet potatoes
big as newborn babies, and discovered
the power of clouds in boilers.
The spring said its diamonds under the poplars
and the spine twinkled like a milkyway.
Children shouted kickball and tag
from early evening until dark in the pasture.
I like to think they found in work
a soil subliminal and sublime.
Their best conspiracies were two
breathing in the night. They lived
on the upland atoll and didn't care
to step on horizons. And left no more
trace than a cloud shadow when I woke
from the coils of the cell's heart,
in the non-euclidean mountains,
recovering pieces of the morgenland.

About the author

Robert Morgan grew up on a small farm near Zir-
conia, in the Blue Ridge Mountains of North Carolina.
He says, "Much of my poetry reflects that background.
I have written many poems about the farm itself, the
mountains, and the processes of nature, as well as the
history, the folklore, of the area." After leaving the farm
at sixteen for college, he was graduated from the Uni-
versity of North Carolina (B.A. 1965, M.F.A. 1968),
and has worked along the way as a salesman, house
painter, farmer, and free-lance writer. He is now
professor of English at Cornell. In addition to three
NEA grants, Morgan has received the *Southern Poetry
Review* Prize and the Eunice Tietjens Award from
Poetry. He has published six books of poetry: *Zirconia
Poems, Red Owl, Land Diving, Trunk & Thicket,
Groundwork,* and *Bronze Age.* He lives in Freeville,
New York.

About the book

At the Edge of the Orchard Country was composed
in Sabon by G & S Typesetters, Inc. of Austin, Texas.
It was printed on 60 lb. Glatfelter Natural and bound by
Malloy Lithographing, Inc. of Ann Arbor, Michigan. Design
by Joyce Kachergis Book Design and Production of
Bynum, North Carolina.

Wesleyan University Press, 1987